BLUE
CHRISTMAS

BLUE
CHRISTMAS

DEVOTIONS of **LIGHT**
IN A SEASON of DARKNESS

TODD OUTCALT

UPPER
ROOM BOOKS®
NASHVILLE

Cover photo: Philip Dyer
Cover design: Jay Smith, Juicebox Designs
Interior design: PerfecType, Nashville, TN

Print ISBN: 978-0-8358-1787-5
Mobi ISBN: 978-0-8358-1788-2
Epub ISBN: 978-0-8358-1789-9

To Tom Heaton

CONTENTS

INTRODUCTION

The light shines in the darkness, and the darkness did
not overcome it.

—JOHN 1:5

A dvent and Christmas are seasons of light, but for those who
live in the northern hemisphere, we also know them as seasons of darkness. During these days the earth is spinning on its
axis, tilting away from the sun, darkening the earth, and conveying that which is cold and distant and dying. But, in fact, that is
why this darkest of seasons was chosen for the celebration of the
Savior's birth—to welcome the light, to offer hope, to serve as a
reminder of the new life that is to come.

And yet . . .

It is also true that many people do not experience the Advent/
Christmas season as a period of joy and light. For many—and perhaps for more of us than would care to admit it—this season transports our greatest fears, losses, realities, and shattered hopes into a
time when most people are singing, socializing, and enjoying life
to the fullest. We may feel even more lost, more abandoned, more
lonely, and more afraid in season—the season of light and love.

So, from the outset, let it be known that this is an honest devotional. Here—in *Blue Christmas*—readers will find these fears and realities named and brought into the light so that we can confront them with grace and truth. Naming brings an understanding that gives us permission to sit with these experiences, to acknowledge what we have lost, and to honor the grace of Jesus who offers us the word, "Blessed are those who mourn, for they will be comforted" (Matt. 5:4).

Yes, there is grief in our lives. There are poverties. There are deaths and losses and inexpressible yearnings for that which we cannot fully name. But if we are willing to acknowledge and walk through these experiences in honesty and with God's help, we may realize the fullest hopes of the season, not through our celebrations and colorful decorations, but by casting our gaze through the darkness to see the approaching light, even if from a great distance.

As I ponder my own journeys through Advent (which are quickly becoming more than I can remember!), I have come to understand that no Christmas celebration offers us a pure experience of hope and joy. Rather, the anticipation of Christmas also awakens other deficiencies and realities that may be suppressed, or perhaps revived, as we experience the stark contrasts of the Christian hope with the realities of the world.

Over the years, for example, I have received a fair number of phone calls informing me that someone in the congregation has died. There have also been tragedies in my own family that have occurred just days before or after Christmas. Likewise, the Advent season is prime time for people to seek counsel for anger, anxiety, depression, or any myriad of family issues that exaggerate our human brokenness.

In addition, many people are working temporary jobs during the holidays and must tread the difficult emotional and financial waters of knowing that income and time are limited. Others are isolated or removed from the people who love them. Illness during the holidays is especially difficult, and those who are receiving chemotherapy, for example, feel sick in body as well as soul.

Toward this end, I hope this devotional and the "Blue Christmas" worship service, prayers, and discussion guide will serve as an honest approach—both in observation and language—to the realities that many people experience during the days surrounding the celebration of Christ's birth. I pray this resource will offer hope for your journey, and that its honesty will serve to awaken new paths of joy and salvation that God can avail to us.

In the journey through Advent and "Blue Christmas," we can all recognize that God accepts our weaknesses and our limitations. God understands our plight, our feelings, and our brokenness. But God offers us, nevertheless, God's amazing love in Christ, who came to save and set us free.

Let us take this Advent and Christmas journey together, knowing that both writer and reader share in these experiences of grief and loss. These are common experiences that can cause us to seek isolation. At times, we may even prefer our solitude to the wild and raucous celebrations that may, in fact, be part of the problem of Christmas, with its overbearing traditions and ubiquitous commercialization. In essence, we desire peace. Quiet. Rest. We yearn for meditation upon the wider hopes and the promises of a beautiful salvation through Emmanuel—*God with us*.

Indeed, not all Christmases are white; some are blue. But all of our Christmases—even the darkest ones—can be filled with honesty and hope if we are willing to first sit in silence with our deepest fears.

HOW TO USE THIS BOOK

Advent is a season of the church year that, for centuries, has been a preparatory period leading up to Christmas Day. In the Western liturgy, Advent begins four Sundays prior to December 25 and was set centuries ago near the winter solstice (December 21), when the sun is at its lowest angle in the northern hemisphere.

Advent has also traditionally marked the beginning of a new church year—the cycle of seasons (such as Epiphany, Lent, Easter, Pentecost, and Kingdomtide). Advent consists of the four weeks leading up to the Christmas celebration.

As with many ancient seasons, Advent has its own set of symbolisms and traditions. The four weeks of Advent have often been marked, for example, by candles representing hope, peace, joy, and love. Other traditions hold that the four candles represent (1) Christ's birth in Bethlehem, (2) his advent into the hearts of believers, (3) his death, and (4) his coming judgment.

This book is designed to offer the reader (and small groups) a devotion for each of the twenty-eight days of Advent and Christmas Day. A scripture selection, meditation, and prayer are included in each of these devotions. Each devotion can be read in just a few minutes, but the intent is for the reader to continue to reflect upon the key aspect of the devotion throughout the day.

Because Christmas falls on a different day of the week each year, readers may use some devotions twice (if needed) or may use two or three devotions to comprise the final week of Advent.

The scripture readings offered in this book may also be explored more fully by opening the Bible and reading the verses that come before and after each quotation.

Subsequent to the devotions, readers will also find a collection of additional prayers that can be used at various times—at waking, before meals, or before bedtime. These prayers can also be shared in small groups.

Congregations large or small may use the additional prayers and the "Blue Christmas" worship services at the end of the book. These prayers and services may be adapted in various ways via the hymn suggestions and readings in order to offer freshness each year. The prayers and worship service give voice to the real experiences and feelings that many cannot speak during the Advent/Christmas season—namely feelings of grief, pain, brokenness, struggle, despair, and/or loneliness. Through these realities, however, the worship service is meant to convey a deep sense of God's grace and presence, and the hope that Christ offers us through his advent into our lives and our world.

Additionally, small groups may use the "Questions for Personal Reflection and Group Study," which may act as a weekly springboard for further reflection or study.

Looking East

> But you, O Lord, do not be far away!
> O my help, come quickly to my aid!
>   —Psalm 22:19

For many years, my wife and I have made an annual vacation to the beach. We enjoy the sun, the freedom, the laid-back atmosphere, and the restful cadences of both music and wave. In the evenings, we always watch the sun set in the west.

Not long ago I came to realize that I prefer sunrises, rising early in the darkness to look east and catch the first fingers of dawn. Indeed, I have always found more honesty in the sunrise than the sunset—beginning in darkness, sometimes in the pangs of sleeplessness or escorted by worry, aware of my feelings as I eagerly await the light.

Advent can be that way too. As the excitement of the season takes hold of children and households, as lights go up on garage doors and pine trees, as shoppers run home with their treasures, I have often felt the heavier weight of darkness. Like many, my

Advent experiences often begin in the dark, with fears and worries seizing hold of my mind and my bank account, the first hints of things to come.

Although I have never suffered from clinical depression, I am aware that Advent can often be a downer. This season often makes me more aware of departed loved ones and the accompanying feelings of sadness and loss. Others in my family have confided that Christmas is their least favorite time of the year. Stresses ramp higher and schedules cram full of parties and commitments, leaving little time to rest in or reflect upon the gifts of God.

What a quandary. And how ironic, given that the season was meant to offer a respite from troubles and issue a call to celebrate the advent of God's grace into the world through the gift of Jesus the Christ.

What do we do?

From the onset, let us be honest and own our feelings. Let us embrace the darkness and live in it while looking east. Looking is key: the anticipation is the sunrise; the promise is the light.

But the darkness is God's gift too. It is part of God's creation, and perhaps the most silent and unassuming of God's blessings. In the darkness there is time to think and time to ponder. We are free to grieve, to pray, to honor what we cannot name. It is okay to sit in silence (another gift).

But still, we look east. God will not delay forever. In time—always—the light will come.

Prayer: *Lord of light and darkness, I begin this Advent journey acknowledging where I am and who I am. I am broken, yes . . . but I am also your child. I am sorrowful, but I am also hopeful. I do not always feel like celebrating or participating in the festivities of the season, but you have promised to be with me always. Thank you for this grace. Help me to look for the light. Amen.*

Humble Beginnings

And being found in human form, he humbled himself and became obedient to the point of death—even death on a cross. Therefore God also highly exalted him and gave him the name that is above every name, so that at the name of Jesus every knee should bend, in heaven and on earth and under the earth, and every tongue should confess that Jesus Christ is Lord, to the glory of God the Father.

—PHILIPPIANS 2:7-11

This passage from Philippians—likely part of an early Christian hymn or confession—is both challenging and comforting. It is challenging because it calls our attention to Jesus and the extraordinary faith he exhibited through his complete submission to God, a humility and faith that resides outside of our abilities and comprehension. The passage is also challenging because it also offers a visionary outcome, one so grand that it seems beyond our human experience.

But the passage may also provide comfort to us once we understand the context, and the thoughts may offer encouragement as we face our own struggles.

First, we cannot forget that, by tradition, the apostle Paul is writing these words under house arrest during a dark time in his life. He had every reason to be pessimistic, but Philippians is one of the most uplifting and encouraging of his writings. When we suffer, Christ offers us himself, and thinking about Christ can be helpful during our dark times.

This passage also reminds us that Christ suffered—that he experienced life's difficulties and hardships—just as we have. Through his suffering he offered himself in humility. It is important to remember that Christ lived a full expression of human existence. He was not free from the trials and hardships of life. His suffering was real, and therefore, he is able to identify with all of our human frailties and sufferings.

The Advent season reminds us that we hold these two realities in tension. We are reminded not only of life's difficulties but also of God's grace, which abides with us through our struggles. It is not up to us to change the world or create new hearts, but we can trust that God knows our every need and will see us through even the most difficult of times.

Prayer: *God of victory, I am often stuck in weakness and stymied in my ability to act. Thank you for embracing me in my pain, my struggles, and even my hopes and dreams. As I focus on Jesus and his humility, may I be encouraged in your amazing grace. Amen.*

Look Inside

The Lord does not see as mortals see; they look on the
outward appearance, but the Lord looks on the heart.

—1 SAMUEL 16:7

A few years ago, I accompanied my father on a series of medical assessments—CAT scans, X-rays, and other interior work that I did not fully comprehend. Afterward, the doctors assessed certain changes inside my father's body, evaluating bones, tissues, organs, and parts I didn't know existed! This interior work was enlightening and impressive. My father and I departed from that series of assessments in awe of our modern science and what doctors could determine by peering inside the human body.

However, we also realized we could not actually see "inside" of a person through God's eyes. God sees beyond the flesh and knows our thoughts, our feelings, our motives, our fears, and our hopes. God knows where and how we are hurting. Likewise, the psalmist once declared, "You perceive my thoughts from afar" (Ps. 139:2).

This dark season of Advent presents us with many challenges. Some of these challenges include fear, loneliness, isolation, or thoughts that remind us of past losses and difficulties. Advent can also magnify these experiences when others are being swept up in the joy and festivities of the season. Lively songs may awaken grief. Sounds and smells may bring back memories of special times that also awaken feelings of loss or loneliness.

Our greatest comfort during these difficult times may be in knowing that God understands. The outward festivities of the season, the bright lights, and the joyous music do not reflect the conflicts and ambiguities of life. But God sees beyond these external trappings and enters into our pain.

Truly, this is the gospel. Even though it is sometimes frightening to discover that God knows all about us—our thoughts, our emotions, our conflicted natures—this is the good news: God is always at work in us and in our seasons.

Indeed, God has not abandoned us to darkness. Rather, God has come near to us in Christ—Emmanuel—which means *God with us*. Although we may be most aware of the fear or loneliness inside us, we need not forget that God lives with us too. We are never truly alone.

Prayer: *Lord, I am not always aware of my feelings and motivations. Sometimes I just feel out of sorts or out of touch. I know I have many conflicts within me. I often live in ambiguity and uncertainty. But thank you for drawing near to me in these dark days and showing me your light. I am truly grateful. In Jesus' name. Amen.*

The 151st Psalm

I called to the Lord out of my distress,
    and he answered me;
The waters closed over me; the deep surrounded me.
    [Yet] deliverance belongs to the Lord.

JONAH 2:1, 5, 9

During my seminary days, I was quite adept at studying languages, including Hebrew and Aramaic. While reading the ancient prophets in one of my classes, the professor pointed out that the second chapter of Jonah is often referred to as the "151st Psalm."

Indeed, Jonah's prayer from the belly of the fish is a wonderful prayer, a psalm rich with sorrow, anguish, thanksgiving, and eventually, a miraculous deliverance. And the book of Jonah, in general, is indicative of many experiences commonly associated with the expressive triumphs and the deep valleys of our human condition.

We may not, at first blush, consider Jonah's prayer as indicative of our human condition, but the prayer seems contemporary, fresh, and deeply personal. Psalms can often strike us in this way, and many of our favorite psalms can become deeply personal prayers.

Considering the "blues" common to Advent and Christmas celebrations, it is no wonder that Jonah speaks to our modern experiences. We too can feel that we are being swept up in waves of loss or sorrow, or feel that our lives have been reduced by the vain idols of celebration and secularism. People of faith may eventually draw into God's grace, give thanks, and acknowledge that deliverance belongs to the Lord. We may also feel angry or depressed as Jonah did, and we may question God's justice and goodness. Like Jonah, we may wonder why God does not comfort us more readily or act more swiftly on our behalf.

Jonah's predicament was one of faith and attitude. He did not feel compelled to reach out to the inhabitants of Nineveh, to offer them God's grace. And when things didn't go his way, Jonah withdrew, feeling isolated and alone.

How similar are the experiences that many of us have during the Advent season! So many people feel overwhelmed, undervalued, and eaten alive by enormous problems and burdens.

Jonah is not a cute children's story, but a most compelling book about our human condition and our feelings of isolation.

Jonah is a wonderful book to read during the Advent season, and his prayer from the belly of the fish may become our prayer too: "I went down to the land whose bars closed upon me forever; yet you brought my life up from the pit, O LORD my God" (Jon. 2:6). Always, the best prayers are the most honest prayers.

Perhaps you have a prayer that you cannot pray. Perhaps there is pain too difficult to express in your own words. But Jonah's prayer may be quite accurate to express your needs.

Remember this: deliverance belongs to the Lord.

Prayer: *O God, out of my own depths I cry out to you and I often wonder if you hear me. Why is there so much pain and anguish in the world, and why do you seem so far from our troubles? And yet, like Jonah, I will also cry out for your grace and mercy. Hear my prayer and give me a new heart to praise you—especially in this season of darkness and anticipation. Amen.*

First Thursday of Advent

Bondage and Freedom

The creation waits with eager longing for the revealing of the children of God; for the creation was subjected to futility, not of its own will, but by the will of the one who subjected it, in hope that the creation itself will be set free from its bondage to decay and will obtain the freedom of the glory of the children of God.

—Romans 8:19-21

I grew up in rural Indiana, and one of the most ubiquitous sights throughout the countryside was decaying barns. Sometimes, even as a child, I would stop to ponder their histories: Why had the barns been built some decades prior? What uses did they serve? Who owned them? Mostly, I was aware that times had changed and that the barns and the farms themselves were no longer viable or as productive as they once had been. Those barns filled me with both sadness and hope.

I always think of old barns whenever I read this passage from Romans, where the apostle Paul refers to the hope that all of

25

creation will one day be set free from bondage and decay—a decay that we know all too well in our modern times, with shifting priorities and the multitude of changes we experience throughout a lifetime.

Yet, this passage also reminds us that change is inevitable. Time cannot stand still. Every person is growing older. Transitions are a part of life. Even our most cherished experiences and traditions eventually change in some way and we are aware of time's incessant march.

Advent reminds us that in the midst of so much decay and transition, we still have a hope in God, who makes all things new, even the creation itself. Renewing transitions and transformations can occur in our hearts, our outlooks, and our attitudes. That is why Advent has always been a season of preparation, anticipation, and hope.

God has created and is creating. And God can do a new work in us too, especially when we are broken or feel that we have outlived our usefulness!

Prayer: *God of all creation, how awesome and wondrous is your work. Although I am aware of time and decay, I am also aware of your new work and your abiding presence. Lift my heart today and lift my eyes to see the beauty of your hand in my life, in my family, and in my blessings. May this day be filled with light and love. Amen.*

First Friday of Advent

Dressing Up

As God's chosen ones, holy and beloved, clothe your-
selves with compassion, kindness, humility, meekness,
and patience.

—COLOSSIANS 3:12

When my daughter was in preschool, she loved to play "dress up." Although a short-lived period of her childhood, these were special times for a father and daughter. I enjoyed helping her dress up for dinner, for those special times when we drank pink lemonade with her dolls or engaged in make-believe conversations. Mostly, I enjoyed fielding my daughter's questions, especially when the conversation turned to some serious matter.

One morning, my daughter asked me, "What color is God?"

Although I didn't have an answer to that question, I did tell her that I believed God is compassionate and loving—attributes that the apostle Paul uses to describe the type of "clothing" that we should seek to display in our own lives.

The season of Advent is a time when we engage in many conversations about family, work, hopes, and dreams. It is also a season when traditional images of God help portray the divine attributes of love, compassion, and mercy.

If we are suffering in any way, these attributes of God can also help us find hope and healing. Clothing ourselves in kindness, meekness, and patience can help alleviate our burdens and fears. The marvel of the season is that we can have conversations with the One who cares for us in the midst of our distress and anguish. God always hears our prayers.

Even a simple prayer will do. And we can always bring our deepest cares into the presence of God.

Prayer: *Dear God, I desire to be fully vested in your love, compassion, and mercy. Although I have many needs in my life, I desire to remain resolute in seeking your kindness. Let your greater love shine through me in this season of darkness. Let your light shine. In Jesus' name. Amen.*

Simplicity

Jesus did this, the first of his signs, in Cana of Galilee, and revealed his glory; and his disciples believed in him.

—JOHN 2:11

I have always appreciated Christ's miracle of turning water into wine for several reasons. First, it is a miracle that, at first glance, seems embarrassing to our modern religious sensibilities. This miracle seems so mundane—or to others, even profane—and yet the miracle is offered as a solution to a practical need. Second, this miracle was one of celebration and joy. Finally, this was a miracle that, according to the Gospel of John, increased the disciples' faith.

I like to consider this miracle during the season of Advent as well. It is a miracle of anticipation and celebration, an affirmation that God is concerned for and found in the smallest of details and responses to human need.

For many people, Advent is the season where energies, joys, and celebrations run at a low ebb. We may feel as though our hopes are running low, or we may feel that our well has run dry. Others may experience Advent as a season of restlessness or questioning. But this gospel narrative addresses those concerns too.

The greatest signs of God's presence are, indeed, noted whenever and wherever we encounter joy and abundance. If our energies are running low, God can be our strength. If we feel we have run out of time, we dare not forget that God is the giver of all good gifts—even life itself. And if we don't feel like celebrating, God gives us the finest gifts anyway.

Often, it is not the extraordinary signs that produce faith, but it is the simple, quiet, even mundane experiences that lead us to grow in faith. God does not give us an extravagant sign, but through the simple reminders of a birth, a song, or the presence of wine we find our help and salvation.

Watch. Wait. Listen.

God is still working and offering the signs of joy that can transform our lives.

Prayer: *Lord of joy and song, thank you for drawing me further along in your amazing grace. I don't seek a sign, but the reminders you offer along the way draw me toward your love. Bless me, that I might be a blessing to others. Amen.*

Second Sunday of Advent

Greater Strength

Finally, be strong in the Lord and in the strength of his power. Put on the whole armor of God.

—Ephesians 6:10-11

People work out their frustrations in many ways. Some of these ways are healthy; some are not. For example, we can pass along our frustrations or place our anxieties upon others, essentially transferring our problems instead of confronting them. We might lash out or transfer our fears. We may find our lives stalled in despair instead of noting the amazing gifts of God that flow into our lives each day.

But we can also work through difficulties in healthy ways, using techniques and practices that are hopeful and healing. We can reach out to a friend. We can listen and talk. We can help others instead of lingering in self-loathing.

Years ago, I discovered that it was essential for me to work through my frustrations and failures if I wanted to help others.

I stayed in covenant with friends. I continued journaling. And I also began exercising.

I learned that having a physical outlet—rather than just an emotional or psychological one—was essential for me to vent my anxieties and stresses. Activity and exercise became a means of grace for me. I know that many others have discovered this same kind of relief through walking or other forms of physical exertion. The physical can impact the spiritual.

Though I cannot overcome all my frustrations by increasing my own strength, exercise has helped me rely upon the strength of God. I have learned that God is my strength and help. Perhaps you have discovered the same in your approach to faith.

Because we live in a world where power and privilege have always been great temptations, we are often compelled to find the source of our strength in fleeting affirmations, or in economic pursuits, or even in position or authority. But in the end, we discover that these sources of strength will not hold up under the greater tensions of the world.

During the Advent season, we often come face-to-face with our own limitations and deficiencies. We discover that we don't have enough strength or stamina or energy to meet all of the demands placed upon us. We can wilt under a barrage of expectations. Or perhaps we become defeated.

Look up! God is our strength and source of hope. Even during the dark days of December, God's strength is sufficient for all of our needs.

Prayer: *O God, you are my source of power when I feel powerless. Thank you for being my rock and shield. Help me to rely upon you when I feel weak and afraid. In Jesus' name. Amen.*

Second Monday of Advent

Expectations

But our citizenship is in heaven, and it is from there
that we are expecting a Savior, the Lord Jesus Christ.
He will transform the body of our humiliation that it
may be conformed to the body of his glory.

—PHILIPPIANS 3:20-21

Expectations are a huge part of the days leading up to Christmas. But expectations can often lead us to feel overwhelmed. Demands, the burdens of others, and our own busy schedules can weigh us down. Indeed, we are citizens of our time, and we often feel that we are living inside an ever-widening circle of stresses that threatens to undo us.

A few years ago, novelist John Grisham wrote a book titled *Skipping Christmas*, a humorous story about a married couple who decided to step off of the holiday merry-go-round and simplify their Christmas celebrations. Perhaps Grisham struck a note here, as many people have wanted to do just that at one time or another: skip Christmas with its myriad of expectations and demands.

But the apostle Paul offers us another take on these expectations. He notes that we are citizens of heaven and that our expectations are bound up in our hope in Jesus. Our expectations can be transformed from pursuits into celebrations. We can, essentially, relax into the grace that God offers us in Christ.

How are you experiencing stresses in your life during this Advent season? Are there too many expectations and not enough celebrations? Are there too many demands that don't lead to hopefulness and joy?

Take a step back today. Breathe deeply. Meditate on the citizenship you have in God's eternal kingdom.

Better yet, take a moment to create your own set of expectations in God. What do you need today? What wonders do you hope God might reveal to you? What blessings? Where might you glimpse the joy and amazing grace evident in this season?

Prayer: *Eternal God, you have always made a way for your people. Today, help me rest in your promises and give up some of my fleeting expectations as I look to your hope and light. I am grateful for these blessings and know that you are with me always. Help me to be a vessel of your peace. Amen.*

Looking Out

> How lonely sits the city that once was full of people!
> How like a widow she has become, she that was great
> among the nations.
>
> —LAMENTATIONS 1:1

The Bible is, if anything, an honest book. The scriptures do not shield us from the realities of death, destruction, war, hunger, and other forms of human misery. But we don't have to open the Bible to connect with these forms of suffering.

We live in an age of information that comes to us second-by-second in the form of image and innuendo. Social media, weather alerts, the availability of the internet, and hundreds of news stations and radio broadcasts keep our eyes and ears filled to overflowing with the latest information from across the street and around the world.

But the news can be debilitating if we allow negativity to have its reign. We may even find ourselves lamenting the state of our neighborhoods, nation, and world.

This season, however, can serve to remind us that we are not in charge of the world. Bad things will, and do, happen. There are many struggles and battles going on—inside and outside—that threaten to undo us.

But regardless of what we see when we look out, we can draw near to the hope that Christ offers us. "What will separate us from the love of God in Christ?" the apostle Paul asks. His answer is a resounding, "Nothing!" (See Romans 8.)

Indeed, Advent is a season of realities and responsibilities. It is a season of hope and hopefulness. God loves the world that God has created and has sent salvation. Even in the midst of dire circumstances, we can look out and watch expectantly for the new thing that God will do.

Live in anticipation today. Keep watch. Wait. Hope. For the Lord is with us!

Prayer: *O God, even when I don't know what to pray, I can always pray this prayer . . . Our Father, who art in heaven, hallowed be thy name . . . Amen.*

New Light

The steadfast love of the LORD never ceases, his mercies never come to an end; they are new every morning; great is your faithfulness.

—LAMENTATIONS 3:22-23

I can remember when the streetlights came to our town. It was 1969, and prior to the installation of the lights, the streets were relatively dark. But the lights changed most everything. In fact, my friends and I would often gather underneath the newly installed streetlight outside of our house on summer nights. The light offered community, conversation, and a sense of security.

The interplay of light and darkness is one of the central themes of Advent, and in times of despair and depression, light can be a most welcome presence. Likewise, just as sunlight is dependable and consistent (the sun always rises!), people of faith regard the light as a sign of God's faithfulness and mercy.

Every day is a gift. We do not create the world or make the sun rise or bring rain upon the earth. These are God's mercies offered to us new each day.

New mornings are gifts that are especially meaningful during times of sadness and grief. God honors our lamentations, our honest feelings, by offering solace in God's constant love. As the apostle Paul notes, nothing can separate us from the love of God in Christ. (See Romans 8.)

Now that we are in the throes of Advent, a time of waiting and watching, we are reminded that God does not heal or encourage us by our effort, nor by our strength. Rather, we rest in the new light that God offers—God's everlasting mercy, which is grace.

As we consider our needs today, rest assured that we can bring our broken places into God's presence. It is not whole people who need God's touch, but the hurting and the hungry.

God's mercies do not end. There is enough grace for today.

Prayer: *Gracious God, I want to rest in your love today. I bring nothing more than my simple faith and my greater need. Heal me where I need to be healed. Touch me where I need to be touched. Restore me where I need to be restored. In your mercy. Amen.*

Second Thursday of Advent

Lessons from the Garden

> The Lord will guide you continually, and satisfy your
> needs in parched places, and make your bones strong;
> and you shall be like a watered garden, like a spring of
> water, whose waters never fail.
>
> —ISAIAH 58:11

My grandfather was a master gardener and his specialty was growing roses. Over the course of a lifetime, he had honed his knowledge and skills to a point where he could ascertain the various needs of his plants. Water, sunlight, fertilizer, pruning— all of these were carefully monitored to bring about the health and vibrancy of his blooms. He left nothing to chance.

There are so many plant and garden metaphors in the Bible, and my grandfather was fond of these too. He was always talking about planting "seeds of faith" or "tending the vineyard." He drew many life lessons from these metaphors and from parables about mustard seeds and trees, thorns, and trees planted by living streams of water.

Advent is not a time when we traditionally think of gardening, but it is a season when many of us bring greenery into our homes. The greenery—trees, holly, garland, mistletoe—reminds us that we expect faith to grow. Although the earth in the northern hemisphere is cold and dry, Advent reminds us that spring lies in wait.

God always wants to do new things in us. The old things are passing away, and the new has come. This is the promise of Christmas.

During this season, we may discover that we too can shed some of our old and brittle selves. We may realize that God is the source of our spiritual and physical nourishment. We may also discover that God is the giver of all good gifts.

God is not through with us. There is still more work left to do.

Prayer: *Dear Lord, may your Spirit continue to refresh me like a stream of living water. Create in me a new heart, O God, and renew an upright and thankful spirit within me. This is my prayer of gratitude. Amen.*

Who Cares?

Are not two sparrows sold for a penny? Yet not one of them will fall to the ground apart from your Father. And even the hairs of your head are counted. So do not be afraid; you are of more value than many sparrows.

—MATTHEW 10:29-31

When I was a teenager, I was fond of using the phrase, "Who cares?" If my parents challenged me to work harder in school, I would often respond with these words. Or if one of my friends pointed out a problem, I gave the same response. My attitude was simply devil-may-care, and I had few worries.

But one afternoon, my mother took me aside and pointed out that she cared! She also asked me to start caring about friends and about outcomes. Gradually, I began to see that others were concerned for my well-being (teachers and coaches included), and that caring was an important ingredient in every aspect of life.

Jesus knows of our tendency to slip into apathy and isolation. Our heavenly Parent cares for us in ways beyond our comprehension, and also knows more about us than we care to admit. This divine care is another word for grace, and our lives are changed when grace becomes the guiding force in our lives.

Who cares? God does.

How remarkable that during a dark season when loneliness, isolation, and despair may hug us a bit more tightly, God's grip is tighter yet! We are not forgotten. We are not alone. There are other people who care about us, and it is an even greater privilege to care about others.

Often, when we reach out to express this care for others, or give God thanks for God's abiding care, we discover that the curtain of despair is lifted, and our attentions and attitudes are turned outward instead of inward.

Who cares? God cares.

Prayer: *Gracious God, how amazing and awesome is your care for me. Help me to turn my focus outward and to display my care for others who may be hurting, lonely, or afraid. Amen.*

Hospitality

> Whoever welcomes you welcomes me, and whoever welcomes me welcomes the one who sent me.
>
> —MATTHEW 10:40

Some years ago, I was returning home from a mission trip with a small group of teenagers when our bus broke down in a small town in Ohio. We looked to be stranded (this was before cell phones!), and no one seemed willing to stop and help a group of sweaty teenagers.

Just before sundown, however, an older couple happened by in a pickup truck. They stopped, inquired about our problems, and offered to put our small group up for the night until the bus could be towed and repaired. The teenagers were elated, but I was filled with gratitude. This couple, through their hospitality, had actually transformed a difficult situation into an adventure in faith.

I have never forgotten their hospitality then, and I try to emulate it now. Welcoming a stranger and helping a person in distress is truly a great joy if we will give hospitality a chance.

We see more examples of hospitality during the days preceding Christmas. For some reason, the spirit of Christ's love seems to be is all the more evident in how people treat one another. People are willing to share gifts, offer abundance, and help.

Advent also offers the opportunity to ponder the many ways that both God and others have welcomed us or offered us friendship. Advent is a wonderful time in which to consider the many ways that teachers, coaches, mentors, coworkers, helpers, or other influential friends have helped transform our lives. We show hospitality by lifting and encouraging those around us.

As we consider these gifts today, perhaps hospitality will be among the most remarkable experiences. God has welcomed us. And what a joy it is to welcome others with this same unconditional extravagance.

Prayer: *Dear Lord, you have welcomed me time and again. You have even promised to abide with me forever. For such a great hospitality, I am grateful. Help me to show this same hospitality toward others I meet during these days before Christmas. I too can welcome the stranger, feed a friend, and make someone's heart glad with love. For it's in your greater love I pray. Amen.*

Third Sunday of Advent

Divine Friendship

He will also strengthen you to the end, so that you may
be blameless on the day of our Lord Jesus Christ. God
is faithful; by him you were called into the fellowship
of his Son, Jesus Christ our Lord.

—1 CORINTHIANS 1:8-9

A few years ago, I set out to write a family memoir. I perused
old journals, sorted photographs, and read excerpts from
diaries. I created a timeline and began to piece together a chro-
nology of events—high and low moments that had defined us as
a family.

I discovered that relating a family history is impossible without also recognizing the enormous impact that friendships play
in our lives. As I began to dredge up facts about my grandparents,
for example, I noted that many of their decisions and impact-
ful life events were shaped by their friends, by both casual and
intentional considerations and conversations that took place.
This influence was made all the more apparent to me since my

grandparents played a large role in their church community, and many of their life decisions were based upon these friendships.

As I thought about my own life, I realized it was much the same for me. Friendships loomed large in my own history and in my future.

What makes Christmas preparations so meaningful—and so painful—for many people is the feeling of loneliness. The frivolities and connections of Christmas can often exacerbate the isolation that many people feel as they consider the friends who are gone, or distant, or those who are perhaps dealing with difficulties of their own.

Our friendships, while a source of enormous comfort, can also create feelings of sadness too.

During these down times, it is especially comforting to recall the divine friendship of Jesus, who draws us into the tether of his love. We are adopted into his family, into his care.

Surely he accepts our sadness and can help us through our difficult days. His friendship is never-ending.

Prayer: *Dear Jesus, thank you for your friendship and for the caring presence you offer day by day. Help me to remember these gifts as I recall friends both near and far. I give thanks for your kindness and mercy. Amen.*

Third Monday of Advent

Waking Up

Jesus said, "Beware, keep alert; for you do not know when the time will come. It is like a man going on a journey, when he leaves home and puts his slaves in charge, each with his work, and commands the doorkeeper to be on the watch. Therefore, keep awake—for you do not know when the master of the house will come, in the evening, or at midnight, or at cockcrow, or at dawn, or else he may find you asleep when he comes suddenly. And what I say to you I say to all: Keep awake."

—Mark 13:33-37

Some people are night people, while others are morning people. Some do their best work by moonlight, while others need the energy of the new day to begin afresh and focus on the tasks at hand. Regardless, there is no doubt that waking in winter is more difficult. Darkness seems to have a firmer hold on our energies and motivations.

Waking is all the more difficult if we are anxious, depressed, angry, or restless. Sleep, then, becomes a sanctuary, a type of fortress that isolates us from the challenges of the day.

Likewise, in our modern age, technology (cell phones, social media, etc.) has had an isolating effect. An increasing number of people seem to live vicariously through technology, and it affects their relationships, their work, and their play. It is more difficult for us to be awake and fully aware of others and our surroundings when our devices hold us hostage. Sometimes we describe this distracted state as "sleepwalking"—people going through the motions of life but without an awareness or focus on the tasks at hand. The average American now spends nearly an hour a day on Facebook or other social media, so it is easy to see how our relationships and face-to-face interactions can suffer.

While Jesus didn't speak to these issues directly, he did implore his followers to stay awake, to be aware. And Jesus describes this awareness as a journey.

We can certainly identify with these concepts in our fast-paced world. So often, we can be oblivious to the wonders around us, or we can miss out on opportunities to be helpful or gracious to others. Likewise, we can fail to see what God is doing if we are too focused on our own problems and personal concerns. Self-absorption and isolation leads to sleep walking. Community and concern for others offers a fully invested and energized life.

Yes, it is still dark. But God is not sleeping. God invites us on the journey of salvation and wholeness, an invitation to see what God can do.

Prayer: *God of glory, I offer you my weariness and my energies, my sleeping and my waking. Bring me to a new awareness of your living presence. Amaze me today! I am eager and watching. Amen.*

Third Tuesday of Advent

Change Is Difficult

In the beginning was the Word, and the Word was with God, and the Word was God. He was in the beginning with God. All things came into being through him, and without him not one thing came into being. What has come into being in him was life, and the life was the light of all people. The light shines in the darkness, and the darkness did not overcome it.

—JOHN 1:1-5

Some years ago, I began taking courses to become a coach-facilitator for pastors and congregations. This training taught me much about listening and how to ask good questions. The training also offered new insights into the human condition, especially related to the struggle people have making difficult decisions.

In one of our sessions, our guide noted that when struggle or anxiety or worry are present in our lives, these difficulties are usually centered upon a change or shift that is altering our perception

49

of ourselves or our world. A change of career, a child's graduation, a move to a new community, a job loss, marriage, divorce, the death of a loved one—all of these situations (and more) represent the many types of changes we are required to navigate in life.

Such changes—even seemingly insignificant ones—can trigger anxiety, worry, or anger.

But change is inevitable. That's one of life's persistent lessons. The world is constantly changing, and the circumstances surrounding our days are always shifting and moving in the flowing sands of time.

However, the good news is that God's presence and work in our lives remains consistent. The beginning of the Gospel of John provides an astounding theology that offers several insights.

First, this Gospel notes that there has always been change. From the very beginning of the universe, the creative energy of God has been forming and reforming the cosmos. This prelude to the Gospel also tells us that darkness has always been present—places and times and actual illimitable space that seems dark and frightening to us. But the prelude also tells us that God's light has always been at work in the darkness, reaching into our fears, illuminating the way, and calling us forward into the loving presence of Creator God.

Such affirmations can change our perceptions and attitudes as well!

In fact, the prelude of John's Gospel is much like a hymn of praise—a word acknowledging the awesome creative power of God, our fear of the darkness and change, and the call to be people of the light. Perhaps, during this "Blue Christmas," we may see this light that shines in the darkness and affirm that even though change is inevitable, we need not fear, for God is with us.

Prayer: *Creator of the universe, how grateful I am that you continue your work of creation in me. Alleviate my fears. Show me your light. Help me walk in the path of peace and truth. Bless me through the many changes I will encounter in the days to come. Through Christ our Lord. Amen.*

Third Wednesday of Advent

Testimony

There was a man sent from God, whose name was John. He came as a witness to testify to the light, so that all might believe through him. He himself was not the light, but he came to testify to the light. The true light, which enlightens everyone, was coming into the world.

—JOHN 1:6-9

I grew up in a small United Methodist church where giving testimonies was customary. Usually, the pastor would call upon two or three people each week to offer a word of thanksgiving or praise. Others gave testimony to God's grace or affirmed that God had helped them through a particular difficulty. Still others testified to the blessings that they had received.

Hearing so many testimonies as a child, I came to realize that everyone has, at one time or another, honored God with thanksgiving or marveled at God's grace. Everyone has a story to tell.

Perhaps our greatest testimonies derive from times of sadness or loss. Often, our most challenging times serve to remind us of

God's strength, or at the very least, cause us to call out to God for help. We are often aware of God's mercy when we need it most.

Following on the heels of the prelude in the Gospel of John, we hear of the testimony of John the Baptizer, who comes to bear witness to the light of Christ. John does not have an easy life. Rather, his way is harsh—a life built in the wilderness of fasting, prayer, and at times, a complete isolation from society. John is not a popular figure so much as a powerful one. He may be more entertainment than inspiration. And yet, his testimony does not point to any of his difficulties, but rather to the powerful spirit of Jesus.

Over the years, I have heard people give their testimonies of God's grace and love, and I recall those that came out of times of deep sadness, distress, or pain. Testimonies of God's triumph over evil, or God's deliverance from depression, or God's presence during times of loss come to mind most frequently.

Likewise, our times of struggle may also provide an opportunity for testimony. If we feel alone, our testimony may be in befriending someone or offering our help to another in need. If we are afraid, our testimony may take the form of stepping out in faith and pressing beyond our comfort zone. If we are experiencing painful memories or feeling sad during the season of Advent, talking to another person about our hopes and dreams may be the perfect testimony—and the most grace-filled response—to our grief.

Our testimonies don't have to be articulate. What matters most is that we see God's grace and love helping us through our tough times.

Prayer: *God of the ages, I know my words ineffectively and inaccurately describe my feelings, but you know all about me and my troubles. I rest in your grace and peace today, and I will look for ways to offer testimony in word and deed to your amazing love. Bless me, that I may be a blessing to others. Amen.*

Seed Faith

The days are surely coming, says the Lᴏʀᴅ, when I will fulfill the promise I made to the house of Israel and the house of Judah. In those days and at that time I will cause a righteous Branch to spring up for David; and he shall execute justice and righteousness in the land. In those days Judah will be saved and Jerusalem will live in safety. And this is the name by which it will be called: "The Lᴏʀᴅ is our righteousness."

—Jᴇʀᴇᴍɪᴀʜ 33:14-16

For centuries, the tree has been used as a metaphor for faith. Trees, for example, have deep roots, which are, in essence, the life source of the whole, and yet the roots remain unseen. Trees also provide beauty and shade. Trees can grow for decades, even centuries, but have small beginnings. And trees provide a home or shelter to many other living things.

Likewise, trees only grow strong as they are exposed to the elements—the harsh forces of nature, the wind, and the rain.

The more a tree struggles for water and sunlight, the higher it reaches and the greater its ultimate strength to withstand seasons of draught or blight.

Some years ago, scientists conducted experiments in a biosphere, planting trees in relatively shallow soil with the hope of learning how to grow plant life for space exploration or in other artificial climates. They discovered that, in the biosphere, the trees grew rapidly in the shallow soil and with the constant attention of caretakers who provided sufficient water and nutrients. But as soon as the trees were exposed to any difficulties, they toppled to the ground.

The prophet Jeremiah envisions a righteous tree, strong and secure, which would spring up from the line of David and provide sanctuary and salvation to the people of Israel—if not all of the nations of the world. What a vision!

But it is no wonder that the prophets, and Jesus also, use the metaphor of the tree to describe the deeper resources of faith.

During the prelude to Christmas, trees often take a prominent place in many homes. Serving as a symbol of life, faith, and salvation, trees are focal points for our Christmas celebrations and anticipations. Like the prophet Jeremiah, we are expecting our salvation to come quickly. We are expecting a light in the darkness, and we continue to hold out hope for peace.

Although we do not usually plant trees in the winter, perhaps we can hold out hope for planting a tree in the spring. Even if we won't be alive to enjoy the full expression of that tree, we can always plant our seeds of faith and hope, trusting that God will allow our efforts to be a blessing to others.

A small seed, especially one planted during a difficult time, may be the greatest expression of our faith.

Prayer: *O God, I know I cannot always see the results of my faith. Some growth takes a lifetime, and some seeds do not immediately take root. Help me to put my whole trust in you, even as I trust that you will give the increase in your time and not my own. I continue to wait upon you, and in your word do I hope. In Jesus' name. Amen.*

Spirit Song

The sun shall no longer be
  your light by day,
nor for brightness shall the moon
  give light to you by night;
but the Lord will be your everlasting light,
  and your God will be your glory.

—Isaiah 60:19

Although my grandmother lived for over a hundred years, she knew no one in the family during her final decade of life. Her dementia was difficult for everyone, and some of our last visits with her consisted of sitting in silence, hopeful that she might be aware of our continued love even as her mind darkened and her voice stilled.

From time to time, however, Grandmother would surprise us. She would sing. And what she sang were familiar hymns.

Amazingly, in spite of her condition, she sang entire hymns from beginning to end. "Jesus Is the Sweetest Name I Know,"

"There's Something about That Name," and "When the Roll Is Called Up Yonder" were some of the songs she could recall in their entirety. The words were of comfort to her and to her family.

Indeed, during the dark days of our lives—times of despair, heartache, anxiety, depression, or grief—we are often comforted by the familiar refrains of poetry or the promises found in song. Familiar Christmas carols can be a source of comfort, but they might also awaken memories of painful loss. And that is why the words can often provide a source of strength. Isaiah's poetry, especially, reminds us of God's shining promises through its beautiful metaphors.

Although scholars don't know much about the prophet Isaiah, most would affirm that, whoever he was, he was certainly one of the greatest poets who ever lived. In the prophet's poetry, we discover words that have inspired musical composers from Handel to Bach. The prophet's words have inspired many a literary work, and the prophet's images have lived on in art and beauty.

Like the other prophets of old, Isaiah does not shy away from speaking to the world's stark realities. The prophet does not paint an image of a cotton-candy world or offer clichés while disregarding the human condition. Rather, he speaks eloquently of the presence of God, offering hope and promise to those walking through dark times.

In many respects, the prophet Isaiah offers a timeless message. Regardless of our circumstances, our defeats, our despair, or our outcomes, God is with us. The light that we celebrate this season is an eternal light. This light is not hidden away for future times. Rather, it is an eternal light that has always shined into the dark times—both personal and social—and is the very light of God's continual presence with us.

Isaiah still speaks to our times and circumstances. He reminds us that beauty and wonder and glory are still evident when God is near.

Prayer: *Glorious God, there are joys and wonders of the season, blessings that you have brought into my life. Even when I am unaware of them, or when my hope has dimmed, come Holy Spirit and encourage me once again with your light. I am grateful for the gifts of family, friendship, and the church. In Jesus' name. Amen.*

Preparing for Joy

May the God of hope fill you with all joy and peace in believing, so that you may abound in hope by the power of the Holy Spirit.

—ROMANS 15:13

Some years ago, I invited people in the congregation to write their testimonies in an Advent guide that we published. The response was overwhelming.

People of all ages came forward to offer their witness. We received stories from children who wanted to tell about a favorite gift they had given. Many parents wrote about cherished memories. Some of our seniors were able to convey their faith through dark times in national or world history. These written devotions impacted our community and our celebration of Christmas.

Reflecting on that little devotional book, I would add that we are often unprepared to receive joy. Sometimes it just appears, unannounced but welcomed, into surprising corners of our lives.

Before my aunt died, she embodied the joy of Christmas. She was always preparing to receive the beautiful Advent surprises, making hearth and home and heart into a place where the Spirit of God could dwell. Through music, art, décor, and so much more, my aunt made joy the focus of the day.

As we reflect on our experiences of the season, we might ask: What is holding us back from receiving God's joy? What barriers are keeping us from experiencing a full measure of the loving Spirit of God?

Let us not delay.

We can move toward this joy in our preparations, in our acknowledgment that all good gifts come from God. We can recognize that God's grace is the most amazing gift of all.

Prayer: *God of grace, move me to joy this day. Create in me a spirit of gratitude and thanksgiving. Help me take inventory of my blessings. By your gracious hand I have received more than I could ever acknowledge. Indeed, you are good all the time. In Jesus' name. Amen.*

God's Help

Why are you cast down, O my soul,
   and why are you disquieted within me?
Hope in God; for I shall again praise him,
   my help and my God.

—PSALM 43:5

Henry Wadsworth Longfellow was a celebrated writer who, at the pinnacle of his career, was affected by the tragic death of his wife in 1861. Subsequently, the Civil War in America began that same year, and the heartache of war was an additional burden for Longfellow. Two years into the war, Longfellow received word that his own son had been seriously wounded during his service in the Army of the Potomac.

That year, as Longfellow sat at his desk on Christmas Day, he heard the church bells ringing in the distance. His heart, though burdened, longed for God's help and peace. When he put pen to paper that day, he wrote the following words, lines that eventually became a beloved Advent carol:

I heard the bells on Christmas Day
Their old familiar carols play,
And wild and sweet
The words repeat
Of peace on earth, good will to men!

I thought how, as the day had come,
The belfries of all Christendom
Had rolled along
The unbroken song
Of peace on earth, good will to men!

Till, ringing, singing on its way,
The world revolved from night to day,
A voice, a chime,
A chant sublime
Of peace on earth, good will to men!

Then from each black, accursed mouth
The cannon thundered in the South,
And with the sound
The carols drowned
Of peace on earth, good will to men!

It was as if an earthquake rent
The hearth-stones of a continent,
And made forlorn
The households born
Of peace on earth, good will to men!

And in despair I bowed my head:
"There is no peace on earth," I said;
"For hate is strong
And mocks the song

Of peace on earth, good will to men."

Then pealed the bells more loud and deep:
"God is not dead, nor doth he sleep!
The wrong shall fail,
The right prevail,
With peace on earth, good will to men!"

Prayer: *God, my life has been affected by many heart-wrenching events and by forces that are beyond my control. Help me not to despair, but to continue to long for your peace in a conflicted world. Nothing is too hard for you, O Lord. Send once again the deep peace of the Holy Spirit and lift me to see the light of your eternity. Amen.*

Pathways

Your word is a lamp to my feet
and a light to my path.

—Psalm 119:105

My wife and I have always enjoyed hiking. Over the years, we have prepared for many a long journey, sometimes with backpacks, supplies, and even maps. A few times we have hiked at night, the pathway darkened among trees or hills. If we have come prepared, we have always been thankful for a flashlight to help guide the way.

Not long ago, I had the opportunity to hike 120 kilometers of the Camino de Santiago in northern Spain, the traditional pilgrimage route of Saint James. It was an arduous journey, physically, but even more so spiritually. And though the path was always clearly marked on the Camino, there remained a sense of seeking the path. I experienced this sense of seeking at various times as I made my way, along with thousands of others, toward the final destination of the great cathedral in Santiago. We were all seekers.

One day on the Camino, after a particularly challenging hike among the hills, darkness was becoming a threat. I had not arrived at my destination for the night, and I was beginning to get worried.

But then I saw the light, a small sign that glowed in the gloom ahead. I was elated. The light of that small sign informed me that I did not have far to go—that a hot shower, a refreshing meal, and a rest awaited at the top of the hill.

That night, lingering over a meal with other pilgrims who were equally as tired and excited as I was, we prayed and read scripture together. Even though we were from different countries and spoke different languages, we shared this experience on the Camino, and it was obvious that we had seen the same light or were eager to find it.

Think about God's light today.

Consider the ways in which you have experienced God's light during this season. Where have you experienced elation when you were tired, discouraged, or worn out? How have others lifted you toward the light of God? What signs have marked your journey, reassuring you that you are on God's path?

Each day, take another step into the light. Christ has already prepared the way.

Prayer: *Gracious God, I know that nothing can separate me from your love, but sometimes you seem so distant and hidden. In fact, I often feel as though I am walking blind. Increase my faith and offer me the encouragement of the Holy Spirit as I stumble through the darkness. Help me find words of comfort for myself, and also words of helpfulness and service that I can offer to others. Amen.*

Fourth Tuesday of Advent

Eternal Light

Jesus said to them, "The light is with you for a little longer. Walk while you have the light, so that the darkness may not overtake you. If you walk in the darkness, you do not know where you are going. While you have the light, believe in the light, so that you may become children of light."

—John 12:35-36

Some years ago, our congregation moved to a new location. This journey was difficult as we packed up and left behind a building that was familiar and beloved, eventually learning how to be the church without walls. We worshiped and served out of makeshift spaces for over a year, making gymnasiums, warehouses, industrial office complexes, and rented rooms our home.

But the congregation was growing, numerically and spiritually, as we worked together to build a new facility and envisioned what God would do upon its completion. We worked hard to meld the past to the present, to bring traditions and gifts into a more glorious future.

However, when our congregation finally moved into the new facility, some of our memories had faded, and this included remembering where we had stored certain items. We had forgotten where we put the hymnals. At one point, we conducted a massive search in a warehouse to find the eternal flame—a small light that, symbolically, burned night and day in the sanctuary as a witness to God's abiding presence. Eventually, we found the eternal light and it once again hangs over the altar.

Searching for this light became a powerful symbol for our congregation. Some began to ask if finding this light was essential; after all, it was only a "thing." Others pondered the significance of purchasing a new light or if we needed a light at all. Still others had no history with the light and probably didn't care either way.

Perhaps the first disciples had these kinds of conversations with Jesus. In the Gospel of John, Christ commonly refers to himself as the light and he asks his followers to walk in the light.

But in our dark times we may wonder: Why is Light (Christ) essential? Why must we seek the Light? What difference does Light make?

In many ways, we are aware that our dark times of doubt and despair become comfortable places. We may even grow to depend upon these down times, believing that they are insurmountable. And the longer we walk in dark places, the more distant the light can seem. We may even arrive at a place where the light itself is but a distant memory, or we may come to believe that it doesn't exist at all.

The Advent journey reminds us that we cannot take the light for granted. Christ is near, and God partners with us, makes covenant with us, and asks us to respond to the light that has come into the world. We may not have to move far, but God does ask us to move, to be bold enough to step out on faith and seek the light.

Even if we are in a dark place this season, Christ reminds us that we can be "children of the light." Our faith—the expressions of our faith in word and in deed—does make a difference. When Christ is with us, we discover that the light has dawned. The old is passing away, and the new light has come into the world.

Prayer: *O God, let me arise this day into your glorious light, which is love, peace, joy, and service. You gave us the light of Christ to be a witness to the world, for Christ did not come to be served, but to serve. And so, in that same spirit, I avail myself to your amazing grace. As I walk in the light, show me the paths that will lead me from the dark places into the illumination of your love. Where I have sinned and fallen, forgive me and lift me. Where I need vision, open my eyes. And where I need to serve, O God, help me to open my hands. In Jesus' name I pray. Amen.*

Overcoming Discouragement

Now the birth of Jesus the Messiah took place in this way. When his mother Mary had been engaged to Joseph, but before they lived together, she was found to be with child from the Holy Spirit. Her husband Joseph, being a righteous man and unwilling to expose her to public disgrace, planned to dismiss her quietly. But just when he had resolved to do this, an angel of the Lord appeared to him in a dream and said, "Joseph, son of David, do not be afraid to take Mary as your wife, for the child conceived in her is from the Holy Spirit. She will bear a son, and you are to name him Jesus, for he will save his people from their sins." All this took place to fulfill what had been spoken by the Lord through the prophet:

"Look, the virgin shall conceive and bear a son, and they shall name him Emmanuel," which means, "God is with us." When Joseph awoke from sleep, he did as the angel of the Lord commanded him; he took her as his wife, but had no marital relations with her until she had borne a son; and he named him Jesus.

—MATTHEW 1:18-25

The circumstances surrounding the birth of Jesus are often viewed through the lenses of gratitude, gift, and at times, quaint ideas about joy and wonder that deprive the gospel of its power to address our human experiences. In short, Christmas celebrations most often skim the surface of the backstory of Christ's coming and focus almost entirely upon the joy of the Messiah's birth.

But upon deeper reflection, we discover a myriad of experiences and attitudes in Joseph and Mary that speak to our human condition. Here, at the beginning of the Gospel of Matthew, we discover how Joseph initially feels about the announcement that his fiancée, Mary, is pregnant.

Joseph is discouraged.

The emotional response is telling. Discouragement is, after all, a reality that we encounter at various junctures of our lives. Especially in seasons of celebration, discouragement can become all the more powerful. When life doesn't turn out the way we thought it would—in marriage, in parenting, in career, in relationships, in finances—we can become discouraged.

Joseph is discouraged.

Struggles in marriage, on the job, or with deteriorating health can reduce our energies to a low ebb. And larger worries, whether focused on the state of the nation, the world, the economy, or even the nightly news, can land us in disappointment or feelings of powerlessness.

Joseph is discouraged.

However, the gospel tells us that we cannot lift ourselves out of our discouragement. We do not have enough energy, resourcefulness, wisdom, or desire to fix our own problems. Rather, the announcement that Joseph receives pertains to God's abiding presence. God does not tell Joseph, "Everything is going to be okay," or "You need to snap out of it and get on with your life." The good news is that God abides in our discouragement and provides meaning through it.

When we are discouraged, this good news can be especially meaningful. Like Joseph, we are invited to wait upon the Lord—to trust that, in time, something marvelous and momentous will take shape out of our sufferings and difficulties. God is not the bearer of bad news but instead brings hope and encouragement. God does not cause our pain but desires to deliver us from it.

This year, consider the hope of Christmas through these fresh eyes, especially through your places of discouragement. God does not leave us to our own ends but can transform a hopeless situation into one filled with grace and love and the very presence of God.

Prayer: *Dear God, I can identify with Joseph and his hesitation and discouragement. I'm no different when it comes to trusting that you care for me through difficult times. Please lift up my low valleys and fill my cup with your Spirit again. And let my gratitude flow out of me in my service and love toward others. In Jesus' name. Amen.*

Fourth Thursday of Advent

The Peace Light

"The people who sat in darkness
    have seen a great light,
and for those who sat in the region and shadow of death
    light has dawned."

—MATTHEW 4:16

A few years ago, our congregation started an Advent tradition with the Peace Light—a flame that is taken from the grotto of the Church of the Nativity in Bethlehem, carried around the world in a miner's lantern, and distributed from church to church and home to home via candlelight. The Peace Light usually arrives at our church a few days before Christmas Eve, and people from the church and community bring their own candles in order to retrieve the flame and carry it back to their homes.

The Peace Light has become a powerful connection in our community, and sharing the light of the one candle produces feelings of solidarity, unity, and support. This experience is especially powerful for those who may be walking through "the shadow of death" or who are experiencing grief in their lives.

When people pick up the Peace Light, we also distribute a small slip of paper with various scripture readings, including the powerful words from the prophet Isaiah, "The people who sat in darkness have seen a great light" (quoted in Matthew, above), and the words of Psalm 23. Here, in this beloved psalm, we find words that have given aid and comfort to millions of people through the centuries—especially during times of loss. The psalmist, like Isaiah, echoes the promise of God's light and comfort when we are walking through the valley of the shadow of death.

Often, we relegate these words to be read only at funerals. However the reference to the "shadow of death" is not a reference to the dead but to the living. We are the ones who are walking through this dark, shadowy valley littered with death and destruction. But the psalmist, the prophet, and the Gospel of Matthew all echo the same promise: Emmanuel, God with us.

We do not need a Peace Light from the grotto of the Church of the Nativity in order to experience God's presence and comfort. God's peace is available to us through the abiding presence of the Holy Spirit who encourages us in our weakness and offers us light during difficult experiences.

God offers us not only the light of Christ but also the lights of unity, support, care, and comfort found in the wonderful gift of the church—the people of God.

During these final days of the Advent season, perhaps we are drawn to these gifts more than any we can find under a tree. These gifts are not seasonal; rather, they are constant and abiding.

May God give us peace through our days, and may Christ's light burn brightly through our care and service to those in need.

Prayer: *The* LORD *is my Shepherd, I shall not want. The* LORD *makes me to lie down in green pastures. The* LORD *leads me beside the still waters. God restores my soul. God guides me along the right paths for God's name's sake. And even though I walk through the dark valley, I won't fear evil, for you are with me. Your rod and staff comfort me. You prepare a table before me in the presence of my enemies and you anoint my head with oil. My cup overflows with joy. Surely your goodness and love will follow me all the days of my life and I will dwell in the house of the* LORD *forever. Amen.* (Based on Psalm 23.)

Fourth Friday of Advent

Peacemakers

He shall judge between the nations,
  and shall arbitrate for many peoples;
they shall beat their swords into plowshares,
  and their spears into pruning hooks;
nation shall not lift up sword against nation,
  neither shall they learn war any more.

—Isaiah 2:4

As a young boy, I had an appetite for history. One summer, my father brought home an intriguing chart, a historical timeline that portrayed the major events that had shaped our world. From the Stone Age and the Sumerian Era to modern-day Europe and beyond, the timeline was a depiction of immense fascination for me. I studied it for hours, attempting to piece together bridges and gaps from human history that would help me make sense of my own experience.

One evening, I recall coming upon a sudden realization as I studied the timeline: so many of the major events that had seemingly shaped our world had begun as conflicts, wars, and epic battles. This dawning also filled me with a sense of dread and removed some of my innocence. I began to wonder why humanity had not discovered a path for lasting peace. I pondered the reasons why human history seemed to be clouded by wars and rumors of wars.

It was about this same time when we began discussing the Vietnam War at school. Our teachers pressed us to offer our opinions about the current events and to discuss how the war overseas was impacting our families and our outlook on the world. It was the era of Walter Cronkite and the Apollo program. Many of us in the classroom simply wanted to know this: *If we can go to the moon, why can't we achieve peace in the world?*

Such questions have always been a part of our human experience. They are questions that continue to keep us up at night and conflict with our attitudes, politics, and faith. Like the prophet Isaiah, who lived during a tumultuous time in Judah's history, war evoked many thoughts and attitudes. People wondered, *Is there any hope?*

What a vision of peace the prophet offers. But it is not just a vision that offers a glimpse to an end of the instruments of warfare. The prophet also sees a transformed world, one in which the instruments of bloodshed and destruction will be gathered up and redeemed for the new purposes of helping and feeding humanity. Likewise, all of the warring tactics and plans of warfare will be discarded as people work together as one, no longer divided by nation, ideology, race, or class.

Perhaps Isaiah's vision seems too heavenly to be realized in the world, but this hope pervades our highest aspirations and our greatest efforts. It is a difficult work to create peace in the human heart or even among small groups of people.

Still, during this season when we celebrate the promise of the Prince of Peace, our prayers rise up before God. We hope that, somehow, God's peace may be realized in our time. We long to be peacemakers and peace builders. We realize our faith involves our hands and feet, as well as our minds and hearts.

As another Advent draws to a close, praying for peace does not fall outside the bounds of our faith. We are still on the journey. But we know that God can always use a few more peacemakers in the world.

Prayer: *O God, you call us to live in these times, and you invite us to demonstrate faith in times such as these. We must confess that the call to peace seems daunting, even impossible, and yet we continue to look to that day when nation shall not rise up against nation and war shall become a distant memory. Let peace begin in our hearts, flow through our hands and efforts, and touch the world with your amazing grace. Encourage us, yet again, when we falter. And teach us to pray . . .*

Our Father . . .

Disparities

> He has brought down the powerful from their thrones,
>   and lifted up the lowly;
> he has filled the hungry with good things,
>   and sent the rich away empty.

—LUKE 1:52-53

For years, our family attended a number of small town festivals that punctuated the calendar and marked the high moments of the year. Every spring, there was a Memorial Day celebration, which back then marked the end of the school year. The Fourth of July celebration, with fireworks, was always a crowd-pleaser. And the annual Labor Day celebration in September marked the beginning of a new school year.

Most of all, our family enjoyed the parades that were always associated with these festivals. There was something wondrous about the cavalcade of antique cars, floats, horses, fire engines, police cars, and marching bands. The parade itself symbolized the passage of time, a way to mark the progression from one season to another.

In many respects, I have always thought of Advent the same way. These twenty-eight days leading up to Christmas have always been a type of parade, a progression of ideas and feelings and emotions. And during those years when our family has experienced a major tragedy or difficulty, the progression of Advent has become all the more meaningful for its signs and symbols.

Advent offers a parade of images—candle, wreath, light, angel, prophet, saint—that can be a source of deep encouragement, particularly at year end. As we look back, we can also look ahead. The parade of Advent is about more than taking stock of our low points, our needs, or even our sins and weaknesses. Advent is a season of God's grace, a time when anticipation and expectation remind us that nothing can separate us from God's love in Christ. Tragedy and despair are not the endings to the year. Instead, we look forward to hope and victory, the triumph of Almighty God.

As you look back, consider how quickly and decisively Advent has passed this year. But also note the interludes of tranquility and peacefulness, the quiet seasons of the soul. Perhaps you will come to conclude that you have not been at a distance, watching this parade go by, but you have been a participant. You are certainly loved and cherished by God.

Your history is God's history. Your faith is important, not only to yourself but also to others. You may discover that even during your times of sadness or loss, you have come into the warm embrace of God's love.

It is not much further to Christmas now. As Advent proclaims throughout the twenty-eight days, Christ has come, and Christ will come again. In fact, he is not far off at all. He is as near as your breath, your sighs, and your deepest desires.

The King of glory is here.

Prayer: *My gracious King, may the meditations of my heart be the door to my life. As this Advent comes to a close, I avail myself to your tender mercies and await with joy and expectation the new thing that you will do in me. The old has passed away; the new has come. I am no longer mine but yours. Lift me up where I am weak. Help me when I fall. And bless me so that I may be a blessing to others. Amen.*

Christmas Day

God's Time

> While they were there, the time came for her to deliver
> her child. And she gave birth to her firstborn son and
> wrapped him in bands of cloth, and laid him in a man-
> ger, because there was no place for them in the inn.
>
> —LUKE 2:6-7

During the months that I was writing this book, I saved this
reflection for Christmas Day, for last. I began writing it during our congregation's annual vacation Bible school in June. And
for good reason.

Spending time with so many children, watching them as they
sang together and played and learned about Jesus, offered many
timeless insights. The greatest insight of all is this: Christmas is
not a day. Christmas, rather, is an experience of God's advent into
the world, of God's deep love for humanity.

Hopefully, we do create space and make an opening for Christ
to dwell. Sometimes we make room for Christ when we open our
hands to help a neighbor. Sometimes we do it when we offer a

word of encouragement. We can also make room for Christ when we make time for children, or when we lay aside our own pursuits and dreams of success to help another person.

Christmas is not a day or a season, but an attitude that can shape our dreams and our outcomes.

No doubt, this Christmas Day is a special moment in your life. Perhaps it will soon be filled with family and gifts and celebrations. You may eat well and enjoy the company of strangers.

But perhaps the day, and the memory of the gift of Jesus Christ, will also carry you through other days when your life doesn't turn out so well, or when you are dealing with large or difficult problems. Christ came into the world to demonstrate God's love, to reveal beyond all doubt that we are loved by the Creator of the universe.

Christmas Day is just one day, but Christ can live within us year-round. Such is the beauty and wonder of Christmas.

May God bless you throughout the year!

Prayer: *O God, what a wonderful day! This Christmas, I thank you for the gift of Jesus and offer myself as a servant. Use me to be a blessing to others. I ask that you fill this day with a sense of your joy and peace, so that I may truly know the power of your love. In Jesus' name. Amen.*

ADDITIONAL PRAYERS

O Come, thou radiant Morning Star,
Again in human darkness shine!
Arise, resplendent from afar!
Assert thy royalty divine!
Thy sway o'er all the earth maintain,
And now begin thy glorious reign. Amen.

                              —a prayer of Charles Wesley

The feast day of your birth resembles you, Lord
Because it brings joy to all humanity.
Old people and infants alike enjoy your day.
Your day is celebrated
from generation to generation.
Kings and emperors may pass away,
And the festivals to commemorate them soon lapse.
But your festival
will be remembered until the end of time.
Your day is a means and a pledge of peace.
At your birth heaven and earth were reconciled,
Since you came from heaven to earth on that day
You forgave our sins and wiped away our guilt.
You gave us so many gifts on the day of your birth:
A treasure chest of spiritual medicines for the sick;

Spiritual light for the blind;
The cup of salvation for the thirsty;
The bread of life for the hungry.
In the winter when trees are bare,
You give us the most succulent spiritual fruit.
In the frost when the earth is barren,
You bring new hope to our souls.
In December when seeds are hidden in the soil,
The staff of life springs forth from the virgin womb.
                    —Saint Ephraim the Syrian (306–373)

Let your goodness Lord appear to us, that we,
made in your image, conform ourselves to it.
In our own strength
we cannot imitate your majesty, power, and wonder
nor is it fitting for us to try.
But your mercy reaches from the heavens
through the clouds to the earth below.
You have come to us as a small child,
but you have brought us the greatest of all gifts,
the gift of eternal love.
Caress us with your tiny hands,
embrace us with your tiny arms
and pierce our hearts with your soft, sweet cries.
                    —Saint Bernard of Clairvaux (1090–1153)

Loving Father, help us remember the birth of Jesus, that we
may share in the song of the angels, the gladness of the shep-
herds, and worship of the wise men.

    Close the door of hate and open the door of love all over
the world. Let kindness come with every gift and good desires

with every greeting. Deliver us from evil by the blessing which Christ brings, and teach us to be merry with clear hearts.

May the Christmas morning make us happy to be thy children, and Christmas evening bring us to our beds with grateful thoughts, forgiving and forgiven, for Jesus' sake. Amen.

—"A Christmas Prayer" by Robert Louis Stevenson

Were earth a thousand times as fair,
Beset with gold and jewels rare,
She yet were far too poor to be
A narrow cradle, Lord, for Thee.

—Martin Luther

The earth has grown old with its burden of care,
But at Christmas it always is young,
The heart of the jewel burns lustrous and fair
And its soul full of music breaks forth on the air,
When the song of the angels is sung.

—Phillips Brooks

Almighty God, give us grace that we may cast away the works of darkness, and put upon us the armor of light, now in the time of this mortal life, in which your Son Jesus Christ came to visit us in great humility; that in the last day, when he shall come again in his glorious Majesty to judge both the living and the dead, we may rise to the life immortal; through him who lives and reigns with you and the Holy Spirit, now and ever. Amen.

—from The Book of Common Prayer

O God, who has made this most hallowed night resplendent with the glory of the true Light, grant that we who have known the mysteries of that Light on earth, may enter into the fullness of his joys in heaven.

—a prayer for Christmas midnight
from the Western Rite

A BLUE CHRISTMAS
WORSHIP SERVICE

The "Blue Christmas" worship service may also be known as the "Longest Night," a gathering on or near December 21. The worship service may be a meaningful part of the Advent season. It may also be offered at other times that are conducive to the needs of the community, or within the traditions and practices of a particular congregation.

This service is especially designed to give voice and hope to those who are grieving, or who are experiencing other types of losses or feelings of exclusion or despondence. The worship service may be offered in a traditional worship space or, where appropriate or helpful, in another space conducive to reflection and prayer.

An Advent wreath may be used if this service is part of the Advent celebrations, or other lights created to make this service meaningful as a longest night remembrance. Traditional and contemporary music selections are offered here, but the worship can also be contoured around the musical gifts of the church or other creative expressions of hope.

Entrance and Call to Worship*

Leader: Gracious God, we acknowledge that this is a season of joy and celebration for many people as we remember the birth of Jesus. But we also acknowledge that these celebrations can ring hollow in our hearts if we are experiencing grief, depression, or pain. We may not feel like joining in the celebration if we are walking in sadness or distress. There are many kinds of losses that trouble us in these days of darkness.

But we ask that you speak to us, O Lord. Speak to us words of comfort, healing, and restoration. Give us hope. In the name of Christ we ask it.

People: Come, Holy Spirit, and comfort us in our afflictions. Reach into our hearts, heal, and restore us. Where we are hurting, comfort us. And where we are experiencing sorrow, show us compassion. Bless us in the night that we may see your light dawning upon us. Amen.

Opening Hymn/Song (All hymn suggestions and numbers are from *The United Methodist Hymnal* and *The Faith We Sing*.)
Precious Lord, Take My Hand (No. 474)
Gather Us In (No. 2236)
God of the Sparrow God of the Whale (No. 122)
In the Bleak Midwinter (No. 221)
Break Forth, O Beauteous Heavenly Light (No. 223)

Scripture Readings (Here, one or more readings may be offered along with these selected verses from Isaiah 43.)

*Permission is granted to reproduce "A Blue Christmas Worship Service" for the purpose of congregational worship.

Do not fear, for I have redeemed you; I have called you by name, you are mine. When you pass through the waters, I will be with you; and through the rivers, they shall not overwhelm you; when you walk through the fire you shall not be burned, and the flame shall not consume you. Because you are precious in my sight, and honored, and I love you, I give people in return for you, nations in exchange for your life. Do not fear, for I am with you.

Thus says the Lord, who makes a way in the sea, a path in the mighty waters. Do not remember the former things or consider the things of old. I am about to do a new thing; now it springs forth, do you not perceive it? I will make a way in the wilderness and rivers in the desert.

For I give water in the wilderness, rivers in the desert, to give drink to my chosen people, the people whom I formed for myself so that they might declare my praise.

Psalm 6

Psalm 34

Psalm 23

Matthew 5:1-12

Matthew 6:25-27

Romans 8:18-27, 31

Prayer

(Here, you may offer a time of silence for the people to present specific prayer requests, either printed on index cards or spoken. Or invite the people to leave their prayer request cards at a designated place. Also, light candles at this time in honor, memory, thanksgiving of persons, and/or light the Advent wreath candles during the silence or accompanied by a scripture reading.)

Prayer Song

> Infant Holy, Infant Lowly (No. 229)
>
> The Friendly Beasts (No. 227)
>
> Amazing Grace (No. 378)
>
> Spirit Song (No. 347)
>
> It Is Well with My Soul (No. 377)
>
> Star-Child (No. 2095)

Prayer and Responses

(The worship leader or pastor may offer selected prayers acknowledging various losses and grief among the congregation. After each sentence prayer, the congregation responds: **Lord, give us your light and your peace.**)

Sermon

(The pastor can offer reflections on one of the scripture selections above or from another selection.)

Invitation to Holy Communion

(The celebrant can use "The Great Thanksgiving for Advent" or this celebration adapted from *The United Methodist Book of Worship*.)

> The Lord be with you.
>
> **And also with you.**
>
> Lift up your hearts.
>
> **We lift them up to the Lord.**
>
> Let us give thanks to the Lord our God.
>
> **It is right to give our thanks and praise.**
>
> It is right, and a good and joyful thing,
>
> > always and everywhere to give thanks to you,
> >
> > Father Almighty, creator of heaven and earth.

From the silence before creation,
    your Word spoke all things into being.
You saw the darkness and called forth the light,
    dividing the day from night,
    and giving each its name and your blessing.
But we abused your blessing and turned away from your
    light, preferring to walk in darkness.
We hid in fear and shame and turned aside from your joys.
Yet still you chose to bless and redeem us.
You sent prophets and teachers and leaders to call us back to
    faithfulness.

And so with your people on earth and all the company of
    heaven we praise your name and join their unending
    hymn:

Holy, holy, holy Lord, God of power and might,
Heaven and earth are full of your glory.
Hosanna in the highest.
Blessed is the One who comes in the name of the Lord.
Hosanna in the highest.

Holy are you and blessed is your Son Jesus Christ.
Born in a dark stable, you brought forth your light
    into the world through the anguish of childbirth,
    you sent your Christ to walk through the pain of this
    world,
    to experience our trials and troubles,
    to know temptation and loneliness and abandonment,
    so that he would know us completely and call us into your
    light.
By the baptism of his suffering, death, and resurrection
    you gave birth to your church,

delivered us from slavery to sin and death,
and made with us a new covenant by water and the Spirit.

On the night in which he gave himself up for us,
he took bread, gave thanks to you, broke the bread,
gave it to his friends and said:
"Take, eat. This is my body which is given for you. Do this in
remembrance of me."

When the supper was over, he took the cup,
gave thanks to you, gave it to his friends, and said:
"Drink from this, all of you; this is my blood of the new
covenant, poured out for you and for many for the
forgiveness of sins. Do this as often as you drink it, in
remembrance of me."

And so, in remembrance of these your mighty acts in Jesus
Christ, we offer ourselves in praise and thanksgiving, as
a holy and living sacrifice, in union with Christ's offering
for us, as we proclaim the mystery of faith:

Christ has died; Christ is risen; Christ will come again.

Pour out your Holy Spirit on us gathered here,
and on these gifts of bread and wine.
Make them be for us the body and blood of Christ,
that we may be for the world the body of Christ,
redeemed by his blood.

By your Spirit, make us one with Christ in his sufferings,
one with each other in mutual love,
and one in ministry to all the world,
until Christ comes in final victory
and we feast at his heavenly banquet.

Through your Son Jesus Christ,
    with the Holy Spirit in your Holy Church,
    all honor and glory is yours, Almighty Father,
    now and forever. **Amen.**

And now, with the confidence of the children of God,
    we pray the prayer that Jesus taught us:

The Lord's Prayer

Songs during Communion (People may come forward at this time to pray, leave prayers of remembrance at the altar, light candles, or engage in other acts of mercy and support.)

Here Is Bread, Here Is Wine (No. 2266)
Water, River, Spirit, Grace (No. 2253)
In Remembrance of Me (No. 2254)
Sing Alleluia to the Lord (No. 2258)
Eat this Bread (No. 628)

Thanksgiving after Communion

All: Lord, although we have walked in darkness, we have seen the great light of your love. Set us free to walk in your peace and venture forth to serve those who are afraid, lonely, despondent, or marginalized. Create in us new hearts to receive mercy and to extend it to others. In Jesus' name. Amen.

The Offering

(Offer special music as people present their gifts. Or invite people to leave their gifts or additional sacrifices of time, talent, and treasure in baskets at the back of the worship area.)

Closing Hymn

What Child Is This (No. 219)
Come, Thou Long Expected Jesus (No. 196)
Spirit, Spirit of Gentleness (No. 2120)
Hymn of Promise (No. 707)

Sending Forth

Let us pray.
Lord, it is night.
The night is for stillness.
Let us be still in the presence of God.
It is night after a long day.
What has been done has been done;
What has not been done has not been done; let it be.
The night is dark.
Let our fears of the darkness and of the world and of our own
    lives rest in you.
The night is quiet.
Let the quietness of your peace enfold us, and all dear to us,
And all who have no peace.
The night heralds the dawn.
Let us look expectantly to a new day, new joys, and new
    possibilities.
In your name we pray. **Amen.**

Postlude or Silence

QUESTIONS FOR PERSONAL REFLECTION AND GROUP STUDY

Week One

1. Why do you think the days preceding Christmas continue to hold such a prominent place in Christian faith?
2. How have you experienced the "blue" side of these celebrations?
3. How can honesty about your feelings and experiences set a different tone for your Advent preparations?
4. What are some realities and attitudes that are difficult to express (or admit) among people of faith?
5. How is hope connected to your brokenness and your honesty with God?

Week Two

1. Where do you see people of faith struggling today?
2. Why do you think many people have abandoned the preparations of Advent in favor of a longer Christmas celebration?
3. How is waiting connected to your Advent hope and to the anticipation of Christmas?
4. What images or symbols of the season are particularly meaningful to you? Why?
5. What are some words that you associate with God's presence?

Week Three

1. Why do you think light is such a prominent image in the Advent season?
2. What are some of your favorite Advent hymns and why?
3. How have you experienced loss and healing in your life?
4. What evidences do you see during this season of God's love for the world?
5. What gives you joy?

Week Four

1. In what ways does God's compassion extend into your personal heartaches and grief?
2. What questions would you ask of God during your seasons of suffering?
3. How are struggle and joy related?
4. In what ways might you see your own struggles reflected in the life and experiences of Jesus?
5. What new actions can you take to make your faith more complete?

For Christmas

1. How can you keep Christmas in your heart all year long?
2. What actions can you take to bring Christ's love to others this year?
3. What do you need to be open to receiving from God?

SCRIPTURE REFERENCES

1 Samuel 16:7

Psalm 22:19

Psalm 43:5

Psalm 119:105

Lamentations 1:1

Lamentations 3:22-23

Isaiah 2:4

Isaiah 58:11

Isaiah 60:19

Jeremiah 33:14-16

Jonah 2:1, 5, 9

Matthew 1:18-25

Matthew 4:16

Matthew 10:29-31

Matthew 10:40

Mark 13:33-37

Luke 1:52-53

Luke 2:6-7

John 1:1-5

John 1:6-9

John 2:11

John 12:35-36

Romans 8:19-21

Romans 15:13

1 Corinthians 1:8-9

Ephesians 6:10-11

Colossians 3:12

Philippians 2:7-11

Philippians 3:20-21

ABOUT THE AUTHOR

Todd Outcalt is a United Methodist pastor and artist who has authored more than thirty-five books, including *Praying Through Cancer* (Upper Room Books), *Common Ground, The Other Jesus, The Healing Touch, The Best Things in Life Are Free,* and eight youth ministry titles published by Abingdon Press. He has written for many diverse publications, including *The Christian Century, The Upper Room, Rev!, Midwest Outdoors, Indy Boomer,* and *Midwest Travel.* Todd has also completed the three great Christian pilgrimages to Jerusalem, Rome, and the Camino de Santiago (Spain). He lives in Brownsburg, Indiana, with his wife and enjoys travel, hiking, and painting.

CPSIA information can be obtained
at www.ICGtesting.com
Printed in the USA
FFHW011917021218

9 780835 817875